W9-AFS-846

CHILDREN'S AND PARENTS SERVICES
PATCHOGUE-MEDFORD LIBRARY

# What Are
# Wheels and Axles?

## by Helen Frost

Consulting Editor: Gail Saunders-Smith, Ph.D.

Consultant: Philip W. Hammer, Ph.D.
Assistant Director of Education
American Institute of Physics

# Pebble Books

an imprint of Capstone Press
Mankato, Minnesota

Pebble Books are published by Capstone Press
151 Good Counsel Drive, P.O. Box 669, Mankato, Minnesota 56002
http://www.capstone-press.com

Copyright © 2001 Capstone Press. All rights reserved.
No part of this book may be reproduced without written permission
from the publisher. The publisher takes no responsibility for the use of any
of the materials or methods described in this book, nor for the products thereof.
Printed in the United States of America.

1 2 3 4 5 6 06 05 04 03 02 01

*Library of Congress Cataloging-in-Publication Data*
Frost, Helen, 1949–
    What are wheels and axles? / by Helen Frost.
    p. cm.—(Looking at simple machines)
    Includes bibliographical references (p. 23) and index.
    ISBN 0-7368-0850-7
    1. Wheels—Juvenile literature. 2. Axles—Juvenile literature.
[1. Wheels. 2. Axles.] I.Title. II. Series.
TJ181.5. F76 2001
621.8'11—dc21

                                                   00-009869

Summary: Simple text and photographs present wheels and axles and their function
as a simple machine.

# Note to Parents and Teachers

The Looking at Simple Machines series supports national science standards for units on understanding work, force, and tools. This book describes wheels and axles and illustrates how they make work easier. The photographs support early readers in understanding the text. This book also introduces early readers to subject-specific vocabulary words, which are defined in the Words to Know section. Early readers may need assistance to read some words and to use the Table of Contents, Words to Know, Read More, Internet Sites, and Index/Word List sections of the book.

# Table of Contents

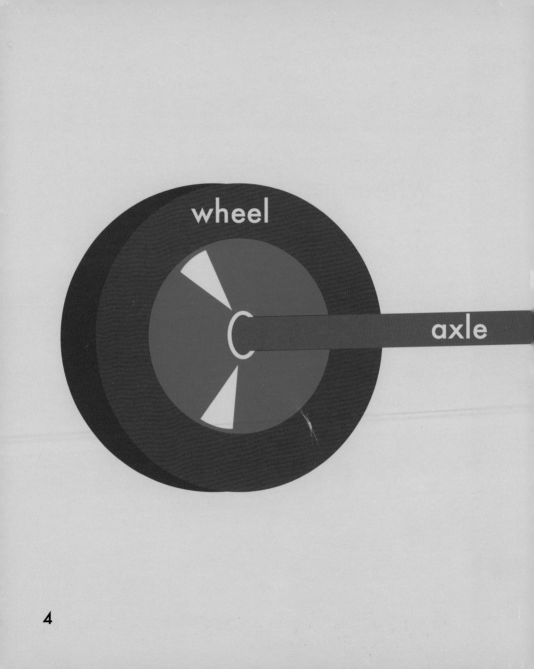

wheel

axle

4

A wheel and axle is
a simple machine.

A wheel is round.

axle

8

An axle is a rod
attached to a wheel.

axle

The axle goes through the center of the wheel.

force

12

The wheel turns when
a force turns the axle.

force

The axle turns when
a force turns the wheel.

A fishing reel is
a wheel and axle.

A windmill is
a wheel and axle.

A doorknob is
a wheel and axle.

# Words to Know

**axle**—a rod attached to the center of a wheel; the wheel and axle turn together; a small force on the wheel changes to a large force on the axle.

**doorknob**—a round handle that is turned to open a door; the knob is a kind of wheel; it is attached to an axle.

**force**—a push or a pull on an object; force makes objects start moving, speed up, change direction, or stop moving.

**reel**—a spool or wheel on which fishing line is wound

**simple machine**—a tool that makes work easier; work is using a force to move an object across a distance; a wheel and axle is an example of a simple machine.

**wheel**—a round object that turns on an axle; a wheel moves a greater distance than an axle; wheels are used to move objects.

**windmill**—a machine powered by the wind

# Read More

**Armentrout, Patricia.** *The Wheel.* Simple Devices. Vero Beach, Fla.: Rourke, 1997.

**Oxlade, Chris.** *Machines.* Young Scientist Concepts and Projects. Milwaukee: Gareth Stevens, 1998.

**Welsbacher, Anne.** *Wheels and Axles.* Understanding Simple Machines. Mankato, Minn.: Bridgestone Books, 2001.

# Internet Sites

**Build a Windmill**
http://www.looklearnanddo.com/documents/projects_windmill.html

**Simple Machines Learning Site**
http://www.coe.uh.edu/archive/science/science_lessons/scienceles1/finalhome.htm

**Wheel and Axle**
http://www.ed.uri.edu/SMART96/ELEMSC/SMARTmachines/wheel.html

# Index/Word List

attached, 9
axle, 5, 9, 11, 13,
    15, 17, 19, 21
center, 11
doorknob, 21
fishing, 17
force, 13, 15
machine, 5
reel, 17

rod, 9
round, 7
simple, 5
through, 11
turns, 13, 15
wheel, 5, 7, 9, 11,
    13, 15, 17, 19, 21
windmill, 19

**Word Count: 70**
**Early-Intervention Level: 10**

**Editorial Credits**
Martha E. H. Rustad, editor; Kia Bielke, cover designer and illustrator; Kimberly
    Danger, photo researcher

**Photo Credits**
Capstone Press/CG Book Printers, 6, 8, 10, 12, 14
David F. Clobes, 20
International Stock/Steve Bly, 16
Unicorn Stock Photos/Wayne Floyd, cover; Deneve Feigh Bunde, 18
Visuals Unlimited/Nancy P. Alexander, 1

The author thanks the children's section staff at the Allen County Public Library
in Fort Wayne, Indiana, for research assistance. The author also thanks Josué
Njock Libii, Ph.D., Associate Professor of Mechanical Engineering at Indiana
University–Purdue University.